Worship Songs & The Law

How Churches Stay Legal
and
How Songwriters Get Paid

STEPHEN ROBERT CASS

An imprint of Solid Walnut Music
15620S. 14th Place
Phoenix, AZ 85048
https://songs4god.net

Send feedback to feedback@songs4god.net

Copyright© 2022 by Stephen Robert Cass

All rights reserved by Solid Walnut Music, who believes in sanctity of copyright. It fuels creativity and diversity, promotes free speech, and helps our culture flourish. Thank you for buying an authorized version of this book, and for not distributing, copying, or reproducing it in any manner without written permission (except for brief quotes). You are supporting Solid Walnut Music to continue to publish books the reader wants.

Printed in the United States of America
10 9 8 7 6 5 4 3 2 1
Library of Congress Cataloging-in-Publication Data
Cass, Stephen Robert
worship songs and the law:
how to keep churches legal
how to get songwriters paid
by Stephen Robert Cass.
1. Cass, Stephen Robert—Copyright law 2. Songwriting

ISBN 978-1-7378891-6-8 (pbk)
ISBN 978-1-7378891-7-5 (audio)
ISBN 978-1-7378891-8-2 (epub, ASIN)
ISBN 978-1-7378891-9-9 (pdf)

Scriptures taken from the HOLY BIBLE, NEW INTERNATIONAL VERSION, Copyright © 1973,1978, 1984 by International Bible Society. Used by permission of Zondervan Publishing House.

All graphics in this book are the sole property of Solid Walnut Music, who reserves all rights. Reproductions for commentary uses are permitted with acknowledgement to Song4God.net Media and Stephen Robert Cass. Any reproduction for the purpose of commerce must have written permission.

Cover design: Songs4God.net Media
Interior layout: Formatted books
Printing in the Unites States: IngramSpark and Amazon KDP

The names of individual products in this book are the sole property of their respective owners

---

Significant discounts for bulk print and e-book sales are available
by emailing steve@songs4god.net or call (480) 773-3484

Contents

Overview and Purpose ix

Chapter 1	Why it Matters.. 1
Chapter 2	Three Revolutionary Changes.............. 13
Chapter 3	What are the Rights of a Songwriter?... 23
Chapter 4	What does a Songwriter Get for a Copyright Registration? 37
Chapter 5	How Public Performance Collection Works 43
Chapter 6	Christian Copyright Solutions 57
Chapter 7	One License 61
Chapter 8	Christian Copyright Licensing International 65

Final Thoughts 73
Endnotes 79
About the Author 85

Titles by Stephen Robert Cass

Fishing in Church: How to Be a
Congregational Songwriter
*A blueprint for learning the craft of congregational
songwriting and getting your songs heard*

The 5 Steps to Get Your Songs Heard
A Congregational Songwriting Plan

The 5 Keys to a Clear Mix: Create YOUR Mix Philosophy
for Christian Artists, Songwriters, and Church Song Mixers

Establishing a Culture of Lead Worshipers:
How to Build a Worship Team
Everyone on the platform is a lead worshiper

The Harmony for Worship Project
Training Voices to Praise the Living God

The Proverbs 27.17 Song Critique Method
The Power of Group Learning to Deliver Songs

For worship songwriters everywhere, that they realize how beautiful their contributions are to the lives of people and to the kingdom of God.

Overview and Purpose

This report is for church leaders and songwriters, or anyone, who wants to understand the process of how churches remain faithful to copyright law. Church leaders must understand why they need to guard their church so it can avert a copyright infringement lawsuit. They can honor songwriters and music publishers, major and independent, with the same action—by purchasing church licenses for song use.

I am also writing for worship songwriters, so they know where and how songs generate royalties and how they can get paid for their work. I will present the journey of a song in a series of five vibrant, progressive, and clear graphics, evolving from copyright registration to agencies that collect fees for the use of songs and their payment of royalties to rights holders. Songwriters and music publishers will visualize how the system generates and distributes their share of song revenue with these simple progressive process charts.

I also designed these graphics for you, church leader, so you can see an overview of how the money your church spends on song licenses is distributed to rights holders.

But I didn't design this report or the illustrations to be so detailed as to paint the entire song royalty fiasco in the US. This information is pared down and *specifically* shaped to show how songs used in church can, do, and should generate income for songwriters and music publishers for the use of their intellectual property (IP).

I am an independent songwriter, musician, music publisher, worship leader, and church planter that has been playing and leading worship in church since 1970. God has been whispering in my ear and filling my dance card with tasks associated with each throughout the years. As an artist and producer with independently published records, I built the label Solid Walnut Music at the turn of this century. We recorded five albums and donated copies to Christian radio stations in fifteen countries.

The task I am undertaking in this report is to help my brothers and sisters in church and music service for the Lord to peek into a black box enigma not well understood and often ignored, but with some urgency needs to be proclaimed. If you lead a church ministry, recognize how your church uses copyrighted songs, and learn how to protect your church.

Support your local and national songwriters by purchasing church song usage licenses. Yes, even the local songwriters from your church can get paid from your contribution.

The story, as it should, begins with Jesus …

Worship Songs
&
The Law

1

Why it Matters

> Then Jesus said to them, *"Give back to Caesar what is Caesar's and to God what is God's."*
>
> — **Mark 12:17**

WHEN YOU READ THE CONTEXT of the above quoted verse, the leaders of the temple were trying to trap Jesus into saying something that would run him afoul of current-day law. They didn't understand his message that *tsadaq* and *mishpat*[1]—to mesh God's character of love, justice, and righteousness into our character and deliver it—governed the balance in all considerations. The leaders of that time were trapped in a world of religious rules and regulations among the conquering Romans who complicated their matters by enslaving and directing their livelihood.

Much is true today in the philosophy of religious leadership. The religious dogma imposed by denominational rules, statements of faith, and resource availability often trap them. And us. Hanging over our heads today, as it was in the time of Jesus, is a dark cloud permeating our senses. We debate following God's law of love and justice because of the daily trap and pull of resources and money. Sometimes the trap paralyzes us. Does God's law win or does the trap? Who is enslaving or directing your livelihood?

> *We debate following God's law of love and justice because of the daily trap and pull of resources and money. Sometimes the trap paralyzes us. Does God's law win or does the trap?*

Instead, Jesus told his trappers that God isn't in charge of the ways of this world, but he needs *us* to *allow* him to be the Lord of our individual hearts for every decision *we* make in the world. Why does this matter? Through us, he wants our free will to dictate courses of action that align with his design for us all: *Shalom*. We are his hands and feet.

Figure 1 – The teachers of the law surrounded by soldiers

Imagine what the response of Jesus would be if we asked him this question today. Would we expect Jesus to denounce and blame our evil captor, or that daily trap and pull of justifying our actions because of resources and money? We humans would just love to blame it on Satan or on someone else. His answer would still be the same to us: God wants *us* to *choose* to align our free will with his to bring shalom to the world.

> *In this case, where we direct the church's money that we manage is a part of how we give back to God what is God's.*

In this case, where we direct the church's money that we manage is a part of how we give back to God what is God's.

THE RELIGIOUS SERVICE EXEMPTION

I begin the critical story of the birth and ramifications of the modern era of church song use in Chapter 2, but first I want to explain a 37-word passage of US Code, Title 17, Chapter 1, Section 110, Item 3. This change in copyright law, this part of the sweeping Copyright Act of 1976, is the driving reason I write to you today. It is often known as the Religious Service Exemption (RSE).

Copyright law in the US is very specific regarding the use of IP in public places. When it comes to songs used in church, it's much better to simplify the message so to clear away any confusion. The passage reads that this is *not* a violation of copyright law:

> *"PERFORMANCE of a nondramatic literary or musical work or of a dramatico-musical work of a religious nature, or DISPLAY of a work,*

in the course of services at a place of worship or other religious assembly."

From the root of understanding that no one in the US can use a copyrighted work in public except the company or person who owns those rights, understand that churches have been given a judicial pass on the infringement of:

- Two (out of six) of the exclusive rights of the copyright holder (performance and display) for
- Two (out of six) categories of copyrighted works[2] (nondramatic literary or music, and dramatico-musical work of a religious nature)

This exemption is granted during one type of event:

- In the course of services at a place of worship or other religious assembly

This means that churches—public spaces—enjoy the freedom of the *live performance*, even if it's pre-recorded, of the music they love, or the recital of poetry or text from books. But not plays or dramatic performances unless they are purely religious.

It also means that they can display the lyrics or text of that work.

To amplify: Churches are exempt from the infringement of two of the exclusive rights given to

> *This means that churches–public spaces–enjoy the freedom of the live performance, even if it's pre-recorded, of the music they love, or the recital of poetry or texts from books. But not plays or dramatic performances unless they are purely religious.*

the copyright holder—to perform and display a work—*in the course of services*. Churches are *not* exempt from any other use of IP or in any other situation.

This report shows why churches should and how they can support songwriters and copyright holders through various types of licenses, each type explained and tied to the reason for it in those 37 words of copyright law. I will describe the purposes of the different copyright licenses that are available from three of the major song licensing agencies in the Christian song world: Christian Copyright Licensing International (CCLI), Christian Copyright Solutions (CCS), and One License (OL). Each company will have its own chapter in this report which is designed as a learning tool for church leadership.

As always, consult an attorney for confirmation of your situation.

THOSE WHO QUESTION THE RSE

My intellect is piqued when I think how some people view song IP usage in church as something not governed by the laws of the land. As if to say *there should be no human laws guiding song usage in church.*

The possibility that churches can be sued for copyright infringement is a crucial risk for church leader policy and procedure owners to ponder. I've actually heard these arguments: *Oh, c'mon. Tell me how many churches have been sued for copyright infringement?* In other words, they are saying, *what's the chance of us getting caught and what are the consequences?* Or *nobody is going to sue churches. Shouldn't they get a free pass?*

These questions:

- *Nobody is going to sue churches*
- *What's the chance of us getting caught? What are the consequences?*
- *How many churches have been sued for copyright infringement?*

... will be answered in the next chapter. Churches of any size should pay attention.

On the argument for *no human laws* and *shouldn't they get a free pass?* I have found no group more vocal than the geniemusic.com website,[3] which in a nutshell argues that church music license collection is against the laws of God from the Old Testament and an abomination. Churches are protected from this tax by *other* laws. It's only money grubbing by CCLI, CCS, OL, and the other song licensers, they say.

The geniemusic website builds quite an extensive argument[4] against the need for any church to compensate for the use of song IP, built around the premise that the US rightfully has written several laws in favor of not getting involved in church matters, beginning with the First Amendment:

> *Congress shall establish no law regarding the establishment of religion or prohibiting its free exercise.*

This argument of pointing to the First Amendment and a misunderstanding of the Title 17 language of current copyright law, coupled with a blanket statement that following the laws of God is paramount to following the laws of man, is tantamount to saying that we should condone theft of

Worship Songs & The Law

> *The infringement exemption law written in the US Code Section 17 is for citizens, not a regulation for churches.*

personal property because of US-sanctioned deference to church matters, and that God somehow applauds the move of common thievery because scripture doesn't specifically say you should pay for IP; that somehow Christians should get a country-club pass on doing what is right by our fellow humans.

This dissent hides behind the spirit and letter of the First Amendment, which simply states that the government will not establish nor intervene in the practice of any religion. The First Amendment does *not* state that a religion gets a free pass on breaking laws in its practice nor on paying its bills.

Geniemusic.com doesn't acknowledge that Jesus and Paul say to pay your taxes and follow the government (Matthew 17:24-27, Mark 12:13-17, Romans 13:1-7). They believe that any law created by the government about church practice *is* intervention, no matter if that practice breaks any other laws.

I contend that this is not a "libertarian" versus "more government" political discourse. I don't buy that the Constitution somehow gives churches this leeway. The infringement exemption law written in US Code Title 17 is for citizens, not a regulation for churches.

No matter where you land on this point of view, I am an advocate for supporting the laws of the land. God established his church on earth through Jesus for the benefit of the sinning public. When humans are involved, there will

> *God established his church on earth through Jesus for the benefit of the sinning public. When humans are involved, there will be missteps and heartache.*

be missteps and heartache. Couple that with the established principles of exchange between humans (the barter system and money) and you have a recipe for laws necessary to protect people and their rights and interests.

WHY IT, INDEED, MATTERS

Let me tell you why I and hundreds of thousands of people across this planet don't believe in thievery of IP and that hardworking songwriters, artists, and music publishers who provide music for churches should be remunerated.

1. Personal or corporate intellectual property is guaranteed, by law, to be protected.
2. Our God supports the paying of a fair wage for work accomplished (Matthew 20:1–16, Luke 10:7, 1 Timothy 5:18).
3. No amount of misinterpretation, misrepresentation, nor justification via the First Amendment and other US laws will change 1 or 2.

Our concern should also be about infringement lawsuit prevention and to protect churches from survival-mode legal tactics from music publishers. Greed happens more often than it should in our crazy world, and innocent or naïve misuses of song IP can happen. If your church is large or a part of a denomination, it has a possible target painted on its back. Suffice it to say that wherever humans are involved—wherever free market economics are involved—there will be self-serving individuals with thoughts of grubbing money. Don't give the greedy ones any opportunities.

Worship Songs & The Law

> *We live together in a land with those who believe and those who don't. And those who would steal and those who won't. And they go to church together!*

Maybe in a perfect world, and certainly in Heaven, we will no longer have a need for the laws of the land. But until our Lord renews this world, there are folks who will knowingly or unknowingly take advantage of others. We live together in a land with those who believe and those who don't. And those who would steal and those who won't. And they go to church together!

There are those who make a living writing songs. Many publisher owners of those songs don't go to church. Church leadership should be aware of the consequences of copyright infringement and the litigation that could come from those who care much less about the spiritual impact of the songs. Even if the song is donated or from a part-time or independent

> *Church leadership should be aware of the consequences of copyright infringement and the litigation that could come from those who care much less about the spiritual impact of the songs.*

songwriter, the worker is due their wage. Not only is it right that a worker receives their wages, but it is also the responsibility of the user of their work to assure collection and delivery of their wages.

Since copyright law eliminates the capture of performance and display royalties for the use of song IP used during services, we, as the church body, should help to pay those songwriters for their hard work. I will show how your church can do this through the purchase of licenses, but first ...

THE NUMBERS

There are over 160,000 churches in North America that have blanket song licensing with CCLI.[5] OL also offers a variety of licenses to over 25,000 churches, retreat centers, schools, and other faith-based organizations around the world.[6] For this illustration, I will state that OL offers licenses to 20,000 churches in North America, a generous estimation given their international reach. If the churches licensed by CCLI and OL have one service each Sunday and they sing four songs each, that is the performance, display, and distribution of 720,000 songs each week.

According to the National Congregational Study Survey, there are an estimated 380,000 churches in the US as of Aug 22, 2020.[7]

There are an estimated 30,000 churches in Canada.[8]

According to the 2010 Census, Mexico has well over 100,000,000 people who align themselves with a Christian religion (82% Catholic).[9] There are upwards of 15,000 Catholic churches in Mexico.[10]

This is a conservative total of 425,000 churches in North America. This might mean that there are 245,000 churches (425,000 minus 180,000) in North America—57.6%—performing, displaying, and distributing 980,000 songs each week *in addition* to the 720,000 songs that are performed, displayed, and distributed but covered by church use licenses.

> *Only 42.4% of North American churches are paying fees to cover their use of song IP.*

To put it in other terms, an estimated 1.7 million songs are performed, displayed, and distributed in North American churches each week. *Only 42.4% of North American churches are paying fees to cover their use of that IP.*

Figure 2 – Praise choir

Even as churches in the US are exempt from the actual performance and display of those works, they are not for the copying and distribution of IP to facilitate the services and other activities. As I mentioned, there is also revenue lost to songwriters and copyright holders because of the RSE.

But this isn't the total picture. The above conservative estimate only refers to churches that use copyrighted music *during* services. CCS provides license to churches for the use of copyrighted songs that are used *outside* of church services (music on hold, coffee shops, youth events, concerts, etc.)[11] They are also in the fight to help churches stay legal and songwriters get paid. They cooperate with CCLI to promote how each organization can help churches. I will tell you how this all comes together in the following pages.

The estimated number of churches that *are* infringing on song copyrights in North America, 57.6%, is a large improvement from 100% as it was in the world in 1976.

I will give you a summary of how we got where we are today with three changes 40 years ago in the US that dictated how churches should handle song IP usage today.

There will be an overview of what is happening with churches and copyright infringement cases, as well as an update on current law practices. I'll also share why the increase of the number of churches supporting song usage beyond 42.4% matters so that rights holders are paid their due, and why it is important to the growth and nourishment of *all* ministries.

2

Three Revolutionary Changes

"You never change things by fighting the existing reality. To change something, build a new model that makes the existing model obsolete."

— **Buckminster Fuller**

THE 1976 COPYRIGHT ACT was a general makeover of the US Code, superseding the entire language of Title 17 of the 1909 version. After the hard work of people over a 12-year period,[1] lawmakers introduced sweeping revisions to copyright law that hadn't much changed since the entrance of the last century.

The new copyright act brought such changes as recognizing multiple forms of media for creation, a Fair Use doctrine, and the concept that a copyright exists when the creation is expressed in a fixed form.

The US Copyright Office devised a method so independent songwriters could have, for the first time in history, federal protection for their work when they registered a song with them. Prior to that time, federal protection was available only to works under an increasingly outdated definition of publication.[2] There were three changes that brought about a revolution in church song usage.

> *The Copyright Act of 1976 and the creation of CCLI in 1984 changed everything for the twenty-first century Christian songwriter.*

1. The Copyright Act of 1976 brought federal protection for independent songwriters,
2. New language in Title 17 for the use of music in church services significantly changed opportunities for smaller and independent music publishers, and
3. The 1984 creation of CCLI ...[3]

... changed everything for the twenty-first century Christian songwriter. These inflection points created the runway lights for how the Christian music publisher, small and large, operates today.

> *These inflection points created the runway lights for how the Christian music publisher, small and large, operates today.*

Figure 3 – The scales of music justice

These events 40 years ago made possible the rise, in part, of the church and independent Christian songwriting communities that we see today (*the Holy Spirit played a part in this, too*). The small-church songwriter will be central to this revolutionary opportunity over the *next* 40 years (see my book *The 5 Steps to Get Your Songs Heard* for a review of this rise of independent worship songwriters around the world and how the contribution of this era, built on the events 40 years ago, paves the way for a small-church songwriting revolution. Go to https://getyoursongsheard.com or https://books2read.com/stephenrobertcass).

Earlier, I mentioned the language in copyright law showing exemption during certain circumstances. Here again is the new language in the 1976 version of Title 17 of copyright law in Chapter 1, Section 110, Item 3. It declares this is *not* a violation of copyright law:

> *"PERFORMANCE of a nondramatic literary or musical work or of a dramatico-musical work of a religious nature, or DISPLAY of a work, in the course of services at a place of worship or other religious assembly."*

This means that churches are exempt from the infringement that performance or the display of works used during services would otherwise cause. No previous language existed, and this new language emboldened music publishers to instigate litigation when churches were found using copyrighted works in other situations. Case in point, F. E. L. Publications sued the Archdiocese of Chicago for $3.1 million in 1984 for the distribution of printed music and lyrics.[4]

Enter Howard Rachinski, a music minister looking to protect his current church and all churches from lawsuits. He founded CCLI in 1984 in response to the new reality that churches could be sued. This legal battle between a church and a music publishing company inspired Rachinski to build a business based on three principles:

1. Since churches were now protected for song use during services, provide legal protection for all churches for their copying and distribution activities. Collect fees from churches and pay the Recording Industry Association of America (RIAA) or their publisher members for that copy activity.

2. From this method of collection, create a way to pay independent Christian music rights holders for their work.
3. Provide a song service for member churches.

Church workers all have copies of songs on their hard drives, in printed and digital forms used for both practice and during church services, and they sometimes distribute audio and visual copies to members.[5]

To amplify: This new law exposed churches to copyright infringement when they copied and distributed works as they *prepared* for their services.

To prevent further lawsuits, CCLI came into agreement with the RIAA and the major music publishers, and they agreed that the payments from CCLI would avert litigation.[6]

> *These licenses cover member churches that copy music and lyrics in preparation for church services. Church workers all have copies of songs on their hard drives, in printed and digital forms used for both practice and during church services, and they sometimes distribute audio and visual copies to members.*

As technology has progressed, churches use video clips of movies during services and stream their worship services, which further distributes the performances and lyrics of copyrighted works. All these situations expose the copyrighted work to infringement. CCLI began by offering the Copyright License, offering broad coverage for lyric storage, projections, song sheets, bulletin inserts, instrumental/vocal arrangements, and service recordings. As the company and technology have evolved, so have their offerings. They offer rehearsal, streaming, and video licenses to cover churches for the use of IP *in the course of services.*

As the last sentence emphasis suggests—and remember that this is the same wording in copyright law—many churches desire the use of music *outside* of services for situations such as music on hold, coffee shops, youth ministry, concerts, retreats, and other gatherings. While CCLI concentrated on offering licenses to protect them for song use during services, and to provide a song service to the worldwide church community, CCS was established to help churches stay legal as they used song IP during these other church events.[7] OL also provides similar licenses to the other companies.[8]

I will outline the licenses that CCS and OL provide in Chapters 6 and 7, respectively, and I will elaborate on the licenses and church services offered by CCLI in Chapter 8.

Other than the legal situations in which each company offers a license to churches, the main differences between the companies are that CCLI provides a song service and other third-party integrations for church services while CCS does not. OL offers usage licenses and then simply provides a library of links to their publisher member websites so licensees can gather available song materials. CCLI and OL pay music publishing companies and independent rights owners directly from the collected license fees, while CCS pays its proceeds to three US Performance Rights Organizations (PROs).[9] I will outline these details in the upcoming chapters.

OTHER LAWSUITS BROUGHT AGAINST CHURCHES AND MINISTRIES

> *Federal copyright law applies the same to churches and companies. Be wise and discuss your song usage with leadership and build your church on solid legal ground.*

Federal copyright law applies the same to churches and companies. Be wise and discuss your song usage with leadership and build your church on solid legal ground. Large churches may weather financial legal storms better and their counsel can afford to offer lower settlements in litigation, but any sort of infringement entanglement could spell doom for medium to smaller churches and ministries.

The creation of CCLI mitigated the activity of lawsuits against churches and ministries for a few years, however they began appearing in the news again at the turn of the century and into the teens. Here are some documented cases:

- 2013 – Yesh Music v Lakewood Church, for the church using a song on a TV show without Yesh Music's permission. Settled out of court.[10]
- 2011 – Yesh Music v First Baptist Church of Smyrna, TN, for streaming two of its songs from their website without their permission. Yesh Music sought $150,000 per song plus legal fees.[11]
- 2002 – Edwards v Church of God in Christ, for recording and selling a soloist's performance from a church service. The court awarded Edwards $1.6 million in damages.[12]
- 2002 – Malaco, Incorporated v Cooper, when a person videotaped four songs from a live

performance and then marketed that tape without the artist's permission. The court awarded the artist $100,000 plus attorney fees.[13]

- 1994 – Meadowgreen Music Company v Voice in the Wilderness Broadcasting, for the willful broadcast of copyrighted works without permission, the court awarded $52,500 plus attorney fees. The station manager pleaded with the judge that the intent was for Christian ministry.[14]
- 1992 – Polygram International Publishing, Inc. v Nevada/TIG, Inc., where a trade show organizer was found liable for unauthorized performances of copyrighted music from exhibitors. Judgement was for $6,000.[15]

NEW SMALL CLAIMS COURT

> *Many infringement claims never see the light of day in court due to the cost of hiring a lawyer and bringing, let me say financing, a lawsuit. But that is changing. We will see more lawsuits because of a newly authorized small claims court for IP cases.*

Many infringement claims never see the light of day in court due to the cost of hiring a lawyer and bringing, let me say financing, a lawsuit. *But that is changing.* We will see more lawsuits because of a newly authorized small claims court for IP cases. The new venue for copyright infringement claims was born during the COVID stimulus release bill in December 2020.[16]

The Copyright Alternative in Small-Claims Enforcement

Act of 2019 (CASE Act) created the Copyright Claims Board (CCB) inside the US Copyright Office. They designed the court to accept less expensive copyright infringement claims with a maximum award of $30,000.[17] The parties can represent themselves, however, it is doubtless there is a substitute for consulting an attorney with any legal action to avoid unforeseen pitfalls during litigation.

The 2019 CASE Act legislation in both the House of Representatives and the Senate stems from research and documentation of frequent infringement activities and remedies since 2011. The resulting CCB creation aims to remove the cost of legal remedy as much as possible so IP rights holders can realize economic justice. The CCB expects to hear cases sometime in 2022.[Ibid]

> *The Copyright Claims Board expects to hear cases sometime in 2022.*

It remains to be seen, but I predict that this will also be a revolutionary change for songwriters and churches.

Decide to keep your church on solid legal ground for the use of song IP.

THE OPPORTUNITY TO FUND MINISTRIES

As mentioned, songwriters and publishers do not receive remuneration because of the church exemption of performance and display in copyright law. The fees from CCLI, CCS, OL, and other licensing entities—all are based upon church attendance—raise funds as a method to also compensate independent—those creators not signed or associated with the RIAA—IP rights holders.

Before I detail how these funds are generated and distributed, see the rights of the songwriter and how they are protected. I will present an overview in colorful graph format of how legal protection and performances generate money that funds ministries and feeds families.

What are the Rights of a Songwriter?

"Music is the universal language of mankind"

— Henry Wadsworth Longfellow

IT'S IMPORTANT TO UNDERSTAND what a songwriter owns. The publishing and marketing rights are inherent to the creation of the song.[1] The only reason they sometimes need a music publisher is to help exploit—find uses for—the song. Music creators don't often understand how to market their songs, and music publishers are in business to do exactly that.

> *It's important to understand what a songwriter owns. The publishing and marketing rights are inherent to the creation of the song. The songwriter owns these rights unless they sign them away in a publishing contract.*

This report does not expand on the relationship between songwriters and music publishers, or the business of the latter, or how songwriters can pursue their own exploitation, except for their roles in sharing revenue. If you'd like more information on the business of music publishers as they exploit songs; if you're interested in the specifics of worship songwriters joining or creating a songwriting organization with like-minded people, please pick up a copy of my book *The 5 Steps to Get Your Songs Heard: A Congregational Songwriting Plan* at https://getyoursongsheard.com or https://books2read.com/stephenrobertcass. There is a detailed blueprint about the business of a faith-based music publisher and their relationship with congregational songwriters.

I bring up this point about song ownership so you get the picture that the songwriter owns these rights unless they sign them away in a publishing contract. Publishers usually ask for 50% of any revenues collected.

Figure 4 – Songwriters

Figure 5 – Performance Arts Copyright Registration

According to US Copyright Law, a song is copyrighted by the creator the moment it is placed in a fixed form.[Ibid] The right to claim copyright ownership, including a list of certain rights, is a moral claim by the author that they own these rights. To preserve these moral claims and to enhance them so the US government guarantees them and their economic expression, they are encouraged to register their works with the US Copyright Office. The type of copyright registration for songs is a Performance Arts copyright registration.

When a creator registers their work in this way, the US government is a witness to their claim of authorship and pledges to guarantee their authorship and publishing rights. The US

> *When a creator registers their work in this way, the US government is a witness to their claim of authorship and pledges to guarantee their authorship and publishing rights. The US Copyright Office will attest to these facts in a court of law should an infringement claim arise.*

Copyright Office will attest to these facts in a court of law should an infringement claim arise.[2]

Copyright registration is required to instigate infringement litigation.[Ibid]

The creator has the sole right to claim or to transfer the work. Transfers are accepted only with the creator's signature.

With a copyright registration, an author has certain exclusive publication rights associated with their work. They have the right to:

- Reproduce
- Distribute
- Create a derivative
- Display
- Perform

> Notes: They also have the exclusive right to reproduce and perform the work in the form of digital transmissions, which is limited to the fixed sounds of a master recording. While this right is important to a copyright holder's income, this addition to copyright law helps to address the nuances of broadcasting and distribution of music in the digital age. This right is not addressed any further in this chapter.

A songwriter/artist also needs to be aware of a portion of their *digital* performance rights so they can manage it. I will briefly address these in Chapter 5 under the heading Worship Songwriter Action List (and these rights are why church licenses for streaming have so many restrictions, as you'll see in the later chapters of this report).

These five exclusive publication rights of the songwriter, as well as the right to transfer the copyright,[Ibid] belong to the creator when the work is documented in a Performance Arts copyright registration. All these exclusive rights are transferable when expressed in writing. The transfer of these rights is the content of a typical songwriting contract with a music publisher, and the publisher will apply for a new Performance Arts copyright registration to reflect the ownership change with the US Copyright Office. They would then be the exclusive owner of the five (six with digital transmission) rights.

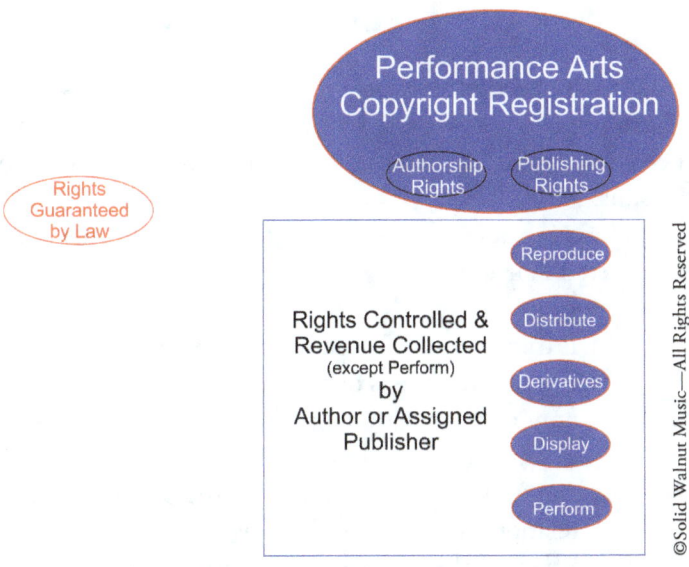

Figure 6 – Form PA copyright registration and inherent publishing rights

WHY ARE THESE RIGHTS IMPORTANT?

The publication rights represent the economic benefits of ownership of the IP. Therefore, the legal "paperwork trail" is critical for music companies and individuals who seek to exploit and protect these rights. However, copyright law also has a provision to use song IP without permission, called the Fair Use doctrine.[3]

> *The publication rights represent the economic benefits of ownership and sole tangible property of the IP.*

THE FAIR USE DOCTRINE

Chapter 1, Section 107 of Title 17 specifies the use and distribution of copyrighted works if there is a legitimate need for education, commentary, research, and similar reasons.

There is a test of four criteria to help determine if it's considered Fair Use:

- Purpose and character of the use, including whether the use is of a commercial nature or is for nonprofit educational purposes
- Nature of the copyrighted work
- Amount and substantiality of the portion used in relation to the copyrighted work
- Effect of the use upon the potential market for or the value of the copyrighted work

The Fair Use doctrine is often first thought of as a defense argument for an infringement claim, but the argument falls apart if there is any monetary gain from the use of the song.

Here's a brief breakdown of each publication right with comments as it can relate to songs used in church:

THE RIGHT TO REPRODUCE THE COPYRIGHTED WORK

The owner of the copyright has exclusive rights to reproduce the work in any form. Musical works have a special provision: The owner of the copyright has first rights to make a recording. After that, anyone can make a recording of their work without permission, but the reproduction requires a fee to be paid for a compulsory license.[4]

The compulsory license payment and authorization are obtained directly from the holder of rights or purchased through mechanical licensing companies such as the Harry Fox Agency, https://harryfox.com, Easy Song, https://easysong.com, or the Mechanical License Collective, https://themlc.com. File a Notice of Intent (NOI), pay the current statutory rate of 9.1 cents per song or 1.75 cents per minute and make as many physical or digital copies as you'd like. The mechanical licensing organizations issue authorizations to duplicate the work and pay songwriters and publishers from the fees they collect.

The following circular explains the NOI procedure: https://www.copyright.gov/circs/circ73.pdf

THE RIGHT TO DISTRIBUTE THE WORK IN VARIOUS FORMS: PRINT, DIGITALLY, PHYSICALLY

The author of a work has the exclusive right to distribute their work. The owner of the copyright can exclusively profit from this distribution, whether through sale, lease, or rental.

When coupled with the exclusive right to reproduce the work, the exclusive right to distribute creates an economic platform for the products of the copyright holder.

Rights holders have complete control over where the product is sold, the price, and how it is distributed. They also have the right to give it to charity.

The Doctrine of First Sale is an important caveat. If a person has purchased a legal copy, they can take your CDs and re-sell them at garages sales if they want.

The courts ruled for restrictions when re-selling digital music files, though. More about that can be found in perusing the Digital Performance Right in Sound Recordings Act of 1995. https://en.wikipedia.org/wiki/Digital_Performance_Right_in_Sound_Recordings_Act

THE RIGHT TO PREPARE DERIVATIVE WORKS

A derivative is a new creation based on a copyrighted work. Sometimes this is called adaptation rights.

Changing the arrangement of the song is one method, but you must get express permission and licensing from the holder of rights.

Beat and rap productions are often based on a derivative work. Although this entire subject is up for debate, what's not up for debate is the exclusive right of the copyright holder to prepare derivative works.

One form of a derivative is a parody. The Fair Use clause allows parodies for educational and commentary nature. But parodies created with the intent of monetary gain require express permission. This is also a fine line that's always in debate. Do some research on Weird Al Yankovic, an artist who has made a living from creating musical parodies, to see how he handles his business.

Copyright protection extends only to the additions or changes of the derivative, not any part of the original work. It's complicated. It extends to all forms of creative works. Making derivatives is quite common.

> *The take-away for songwriters: Understand that no one may change your copyrighted work without permission. If you sign a publishing contract, this right becomes theirs.*

The take-away for songwriters: Understand that no one may change your copyrighted work without permission. If you sign a publishing contract, this right becomes theirs.

CHURCH USE AND DERIVATIVES

Changing the arrangement on a copyrighted song and performing it at church may, in fact, be preparing a derivative. But performing copyrighted songs in church during services is not an infringement of rights. Under any other circumstance, it would be viewed as a published derivative, including the new arrangement of a song the church band performed *outside* of services.

Churches are also exempt from infringement for the display of copyrighted lyrics during services. *However, displaying a changed lyric in churches* is *an infringement.* That's a derivative of that lyric, the sole right of the copyright holder.

> *Displaying a changed lyric in church is an infringement. That's a derivative of that lyric and the sole right of the copyright holder.*

An example is John Mark McMillan's song *How He Loves*. David Crowder contacted John and received permission to change the lyric "sloppy wet kiss" to "unforeseen kiss."[5] (There are links with excellent explanations from both David and Mark in the Endnotes section.) David recorded it, and several other artists covered it after that. Legally, these are the only two forms of the lyric than can be projected in churches.

THE RIGHT TO DISPLAY THE WORK PUBLICLY

The holder of the copyright has the exclusive right to display the work in public, or to give others the right. In music, the lyrics are a part of the underlying work, and so the holder of the publishing rights is the only party allowed to distribute and display them.

Like the right to perform, a legal owner of a purchased copy can display the work—in a single location. They can't publish it, as in post it on the internet, without a license or permission to do so.

How about when Google displays song lyrics? They pay copyright holders for the right through a third party, the company Lyric Find. Other lyric services on the internet, such as Genius, pay the holder of rights as well (there is also some nice reading on this in the Endnotes section).[6]

YOUTUBE AND OTHER INTERNET VIDEOS

Videos on the internet often contain both a copyrighted sound recording and lyrics. Since both are exclusive rights of the copyright holder, YouTube generates money from advertisements so rights holders can be paid. They pay them according to the number of estimated replays. Sometimes the copyright holder requests Google to remove the video regardless, which is their right.[7]

YouTube and other platforms review all uploads. When you upload a video, Google will determine whether the content is Fair Use and if they will add advertising. If the video contains partial clips of copyrighted works, the channel owner could choose not to monetize the video. YouTube will notify the channel owner if the video is not eligible for monetization because of copyrighted material. If the content on the YouTube channel is strictly the owner's own creation, the owner can monetize it.

HOUSES OF WORSHIP AND YOUTUBE VIDEOS

As stated, houses of worship are exempt from copyright law for the display of lyrics during the course of services. They may be exempt from the display of lyrics, but not from the use of the sound recording in a YouTube video. In addition, they can only use the video as a public display if it comes from a monetized channel *or* they have received written authorization from the holder of rights.[Ibid]

The bottom line is that it is wise to stay away from YouTube for use in church unless you have written permission from the copyright holder.

> *It's wise to stay away from YouTube for use in church unless you have written permission from the copyright holder.*

DO CHURCHES PAY LYRIC DISPLAY FEES?

> *Churches are exempt from the law for the display of copyrighted works during services. However, they do need to store a copy and distribute copies of the lyric—both needed functions in the preparation of displaying it in services—but are not exempt from the law in those activities.*

No. Churches are exempt from the law for the display of copyrighted works during services. However, they *do* need to store a copy and distribute copies of the lyric—both needed functions in the preparation of displaying it in services—but are not exempt from the law in those activities.

THE RIGHT TO PERFORM THE WORK PUBLICLY

The copyright holder has the exclusive right to public performance. This is often the most lucrative income potential for songwriters.

A performance is any actual or broadcast performance of the work. This does not apply when performing for family and friends. But when you put flyers out and invite people to come hear you, or a publisher advertises a concert in any size venue, you can document the performance and submit it for credit (more about that in Chapter 5).

Performances of a copyrighted work, whether an original song from an artist or when musicians are "covering" a song not written by them, can generate significant income for the copyright holder and songwriter.

> *Performances of a copyrighted work, whether an original song from an artist or when musicians are "covering" a song not written by them, can generate significant income for the copyright holder and songwriter.*

DO CHURCHES PAY PERFORMANCE FEES?

Even though churches are exempt from paying performance fees to authorities in the US, they pay the holders of rights for the performances of their works by purchasing church licenses from CCLI, CCS, OL, and other church licensing organizations. See how these organizations collect and distribute funds in upcoming chapters.

4

What does a Songwriter Get for a Copyright Registration?

"It is the spirit and not the form of law that keeps justice alive."

— **Earl Warren**

Figure 7 – Listening to copyrighted songs

NOW THAT YOU KNOW a bit about each publishing right, what does the copyright holder get when they register for a US Copyright?

1. A signed Certificate of Registration with a registration number and effective date of registration. This constitutes a legal witness from a government institution of your authorship and ownership of all publishing rights.

2. *Prima facie* (face value) evidence of the validity of the copyright and the facts on the certificate if registered within five years of publication.

   a. If the song is registered within three months of the date of authorship, you're automatically eligible to receive statutory damages and legal fees from any infringer.

   b. There's no automatic right to receive the damages and fees if the song is registered at a date later than three months. This doesn't preclude the possibility that a judge might not see your side of the story.

3. The work is protected for the life of the author plus seventy years (a part of US copyright law, not a specific right from the US Copyright Office. This part of the law is sealed in the eyes of the court when you register your song).

The above benefits are taken from the *Copyright Basics Circular*.[1]

If you decide that someone has copied your work and made money, you're in a much better position to take them to court. The government circular on copyright states that having a registration is a *requirement* before you can begin litigation.

THE POOR MAN'S COPYRIGHT

If you don't have a registration, do you have proof that the underlying creation, the words and music, is your work? Will a "poor man's copyright" work (mailing yourself a copy so it has a date stamped on the envelope)?

Nope.

This method will not persuade a judge because dates can be faked, according to numerous sources. The FAQ page at the US Copyright Office says it is *not* a substitute for a registration.[2] What if the date is verified by a third party? Other copyright registration firms do this. They are in business to make this proof-of-date stamping, like what is intended with the "poor man's copyright," legitimate. Do these firms, with a product often referred to as an "internet copyright," provide good enough protection for a court of law?

> *Do these firms that are in business to make proof-of-date stamping for your song, with a product often referred to as an "internet copyright," provide good enough protection for a court of law? No.*

No. Do they provide a legal date stamp of your work? Yes ... but that may only be useful if a judge agrees that piece of evidence is valid for your particular case. You see, these other firms are literally banking on the first chapter of copyright law, which states that you have a legal copyright when you place it in a fixed form. Their opinion is that's enough. Period. No other proof is necessary, they say, because the rest of the laws are scare tactics. Or the government is trying to make money.

> These other firms are the ones trying to make that money, and the return on your investment is not good.

These *other firms* are the ones trying to make that money, and the return on your investment is not good.

All of them may be good for creating a date stamp of your work, and that work and date stamp is hosted by them, an eye witness for your court case. But ...

- Will they be present in court when you need them?
- Do they guarantee the judge will see your claim of authorship as legitimate?
- Can they guarantee the infringer must pay statutory damages and legal fees?

Good questions to ask them. Do the right research before sending your money anywhere. Read their fine print. *In every case*, their fine print will state that their service is not a substitute for a copyright registration from the US Copyright Office.

LIFE OF THE AUTHOR PLUS 70 YEARS

My answer to the above three questions is "No." These companies all fall short of the protection provided by the US Copyright Office. They do not offer monetary or ownership protection. US copyright law states the rightful owner of the copyright has protection under the law for the life of the author plus 70 years.[3] Are you willing to go bargain hunting to shop for "copyright protection"—gambling with this guarantee under the law—at another business when you understand the government option?

What happens when, not if, these companies go out of business?

Are you willing to forego the statutory life-of-the-author-plus-70-years clause, over saving a few dollars?

> Note: Again, the 70-year clause is a section of US copyright law. But the timely registration of your song with them guarantees not only the right for you to claim statutory damages and legal fees, but it also cements this 70-year clause in your favor in the eyes of a judge. If you allow another party to register a claim on your song, they get the 70-year guarantee.[Ibid]

Here's what the US Copyright Office will not do for you: They will not put up the money so you can begin your case. That's all on you.

Here's what the US Copyright Office will *not* do for you: They will not put up the money so you can begin your case. That's all on you. If you've filed a timely registration with them, you can recover statutory damages and fees, and then pay off your lawyers.

5

How Public Performance Collection Works

"Ensuring that your information is listed correctly everywhere is the best way to get paid properly for your songs."

— **Melanie Lane, music industry consultant**

THE PUBLISHER, OR THE INDIVIDUAL, owns the exclusive rights to public performance or digital transmission (a special consideration of performance) of their work. They legally control the terms of those rights.

However, they do not control or initiate the fees charged or the money collected when those rights are exercised. Performance Rights Organizations (PROs) manage public performance money in the US. Copyright law in the US mandates the collection of performance fees by the PROs.[1] Two of them, the American Society of Composers, Authors and Publishers (ASCAP) and Broadcast Music Incorporated (BMI), are nonprofit. Society of European Stage Authors and Composers (SESAC) and Global Music Rights (GMR) are for-profit with membership by invitation only.

There is a new US PRO as of 2019, AllTrack, built specifically for independent music creators. It boasts that the member automatically receives royalties from over 120 countries using a special digital platform.

SoundExchange is also a PRO mandated by US Congress,[2] but strictly for the collection and distribution of fees and royalties for the performances of digital sound recordings. It is an organization where you register your works, however, it is not the same as the others. The others might offer both digital and non-digital royalty collections, but SoundExchange only offers the collection of digital.

Each country has its own PRO. In most other countries, the PRO collects all forms of fees and royalties. But in the US, only public performance fees are collected, and royalties distributed. The PROs in the US issue licenses to restaurants, bars and clubs, performance venues of different sizes, malls and office buildings that play Muzak, etc. The fees paid depend on the size of a place, the occupancy, and how often and how many works are performed.

> *The money the PROs collect is split 50/50, by law, to the songwriter of record and to the publisher of record.*

The money the PROs collect is split 50/50, by law, to the songwriter of record and to the publisher of record.

How do they know who these people are? The holder of the copyright must register their songs with them. If you have a signed contract with a publisher, that company will register the song (or re-register the song) with your PRO. They'll document you as the author and the company as the publisher of record. For anyone who is self-published, it's your responsibility

Worship Songs & The Law

> *The industry speaks about the performance royalty split this way: There are two pies. The first whole pie is authorship. You and your co-writers own 100% of the pie. The second whole pie is money generated by publishing rights. You and your co-writers own 100% of that pie, too.*

to register the song as the author *and* as the publisher of record.

The funds collected by the PRO are divvied up and distributed directly to the author and the publisher of record separately.[3] The PRO will distribute after subtracting their fees. For example, ASCAP reports that on the average they returned 90% of all monies collected to songwriters and publishers.[4]

The industry speaks about the performance royalty split this way: There are two pies. The first whole pie is authorship. You and your co-writers own 100% of the pie. The second whole pie is money generated by publishing rights. You and your co-writers own 100% of that pie, too.

SIGN UP WITH A PRO

You would be leaving money on the table if you did not register your songs with a PRO. If your songs generate interest and are performed or recorded by others, they need to be registered with a PRO so performance credits can be calculated.

> *You would be leaving money on the table if you did not register your songs with a PRO.*

Sign up today with ASCAP, BMI, SESAC or AllTrack. It's very simple—pick one. You can only sign up with one of the PROs as a writer. Each organization has its own membership criteria. Music publishing companies can sign up with all the PROs because they sign writers who are members of each of them. Signing up with the PRO as a songwriter and publisher is recommended. The reason is that you control the publishing on your songs. When you register them as both the songwriter and publisher, you'll be able to collect both royalty payments. A new development to this industry practice is that AllTrack automatically signs you up for both if you're a self-published writer.

> *While venues are responsible for paying fees to the PROs, you (or your publisher) are responsible for reporting your songs to them to get credit.*

While venues are responsible for paying fees to the PROs, you (or your publisher) are responsible for reporting your songs to them to get credit.

WHICH PRO?

Register your songs to be ready to receive performance royalties. Pick a PRO and sign up with one today. ASCAP allows it and recommends it. BMI says, "Don't bother until you can prove performances." And SESAC says, "Do it. Do you know that we'll pay royalties no matter the public venue where your

> *And SESAC says, "Do it. Do you know that we'll pay royalties no matter the public venue where your song is performed? All you need to do is report it."*

song is performed? All you need to do is report it." AllTrack clearly wants to sign new talent. GMR isn't talking. They are a more closed society for industry professionals.

If you're performing your own material in front of increasingly larger crowds, you should consider becoming a member of one of the PROs and register your songs with them. You can report these performances to your PRO and receive credit.

Here's a list of the PROs in the US:

- ASCAP
- BMI
- SESAC
- GMR
- AllTrack
- SoundExchange

SoundExchange—and remember that you can only register *sound recordings* with them—only collects and distributes revenue generated by non-interactive digital services (e.g., you can't decide what is played next: Satellite, Sirius XM, Pandora, etc.) AllTrack advertises that they track plays and collect revenue from digital streaming companies like Spotify, Apple Music, YouTube, Rhapsody, etc., a first among US PROs. Streaming is considered performance. The royalties are split 50/50 between mechanical (the reproduction of a work whether it is physical or digital) and performance.

The streaming services pay the publishing companies through the Harry Fox Agency and directly to independent songwriters.

The Music Modernization Act of 2018 mandated the creation of a central database to identify and match sound recordings to rights holders so they can be paid mechanical royalties.[5] The database is being built and managed by the MLC, which was funded by the digital music services, and has been in place since January 1, 2021.[6] They collect fees from streaming services and distribute them to independent songwriters directly, while the Harry Fox Agency collects and distributes for larger music companies.

> *A change in US law, effective January 1, 2021, is the creation of the Mechanical License Collective (MLC).*

The effect of this new law is to simplify the fees collected and royalties paid for mechanical licensing and digital transmissions of songs.

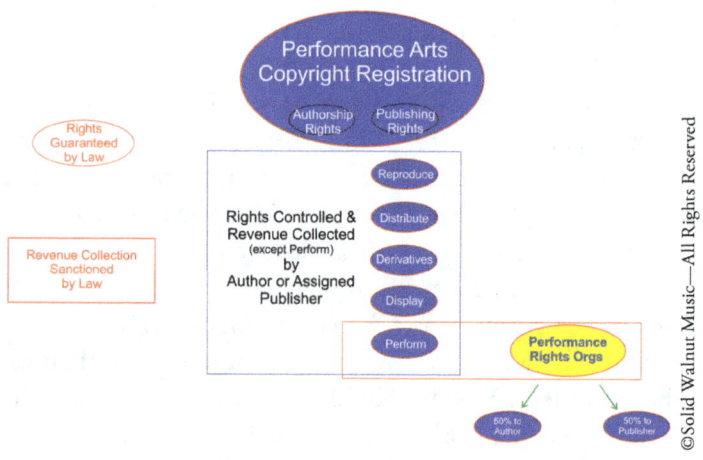

Figure 8 – Performance income distribution

PRO FOR CHRISTIAN MUSIC

Christian songwriters have an additional organization where they can register and from where they can receive royalty payments: CCLI. But they are not a PRO, they are a service organization that collects revenue from churches copying, displaying, distributing, and streaming IP. As mentioned earlier, there is also another major licensing organization, CCS. They collect fees from churches for the use of songs *outside* of services. They pay the proceeds to three PROs in the US—ASCAP, BMI, and SESAC—who in turn distribute the monies to their affiliated writers and publishers.[7]

> *Christian songwriters have an additional organization where they can register and from where they can receive royalty payments: CCLI.*

Yet another important reason to choose and sign up with a PRO.

If you are congregational songwriter in the US, I suggest choosing one of those three PROs.

So, to recap: In the US, songwriters can register with and receive performance royalty payments from one of the PROs and from CCLI. CCS licenses churches and sends money to ASCAP, BMI, and SESAC from their license fee income for eventual distribution to rights holders.

There are multiple song licensing entities that will issue licenses for the use of songs. Many publishers, large and small, have their own, or associate with, song licensing companies. One of the largest aside from CCLI and CCS is OL who collect fees on behalf of their member publishers. I devote the next three chapters to the capabilities of these three companies.

WORSHIP SONGWRITER ACTION LIST

Here's how to prepare and register now for royalty payments. Do this *today*.

- Place all your songs in a spreadsheet with information such as:
    - Song name
    - Co-writer names
    - Songwriter split percentages (ownership)
    - Songwriter PRO affiliation
    - All IPI numbers (Interested Party Information given to songwriters, composers, and publishers issued by PROs)
    - ISWC (International Standard Musical Code) and ISRC (International Standard Recording Code) numbers
    - CCLI song number

This spreadsheet is the beginning of your song catalog. Your next set of actions:

- *Sign up with a PRO to capture any public performances of your works* and to be prepared for others to record and perform your work. You should choose ASCAP, BMI, or SESAC if you are a congregational songwriter in the US. CCS collects money for your songs used outside of church services and pays them directly to those three PROs, who in turn pays their songwriting and publishing affiliates.
- *Sign up with SoundExchange and list any sound recordings you own.* If you have a record contract,

the company owns these sound recordings (that is, unless you have another deal) and will register the works.
- *List your digital works with streaming services.* This is done automatically with CDBaby, Spotify, and whatever company you choose when you send your works for duplication or digital distribution.
- *Obtain ISRC numbers independently or from those who distribute your digital recording, and ISWC numbers independently or from your PRO* as you register the work. You'll need these numbers for the next step. Here's a great site explaining these codes. https://blog.songtradr.com/what-are-iswcisrc-codes-and-how-do-i-get-them/
- *Become a member of a Digital Rights Reproduction Collection Agency (DRCA)* such as Audiam, TuneCore, CDBabyPro, or Songtrust. These are also known as Mechanical Rights Organizations (MROs). MROs are in business to offer song publishing administration agreements, but they also collect and register the meta data of your works for a central database. The important reason to sign up with a DRCA/MRO is that you'll register your ISRC numbers with them so they can collect and distribute royalties for the underlying composition, for your authorship. Remember, you don't receive money from these entities for sales, you receive royalties from these companies because of the number of *replications*.

If you're in the US, you can sign up with the MLC, also an MRO, instead of a DRCA. It's either the MLC or one of the DRCAs, not both. Here are the major differences:

- The MLC only covers collecting and distributing streaming royalties in the US
- The MLC is absolutely free of charge
- Other DRCAs collect streaming royalties internationally, including the US
- Other DRCAs have fees and take a percentage of any royalty money received for their services
- Both services collect the meta data of your work for The Public Work Search database managed by the MLC

Notes: Just to be clear, as an artist, you choose some company like DistroKid or CDBaby to distribute your digital product. The royalties you collect from them are from the *sales* of your product only. CDBaby and TuneCore *also* have DRCA sign-ups for the collection of mechanical streaming and download fees from Spotify, Apple Music, Rhapsody, and others. You'll recognize this from the terms CDBabyPro and TuneCore Publishing. They're selling you extra publishing administration services. These services pay royalties to rights holders for the underlying composition (authorship) related to the number of *replications*.

As a scenario, choose CDBaby for creating and hosting the song only. Then choose Songtrust as a publishing administration firm and a DRCA for that song (or choose the MLC for the song instead of the DRCA, Songtrust).

> More Notes: As your song list grows, the above is a good exercise in helping you organize and update your catalog. Though it's confusing at first, it's also excellent knowledge about the type of royalties payable to you. Don't get caught up in the *Fear of Missing Out (FOMO)*.

Make the DRCA decision with a clear head according to your goals and desires. You'll want to sign up with one of the DRCAs listed if you are an artist or songwriter with a worldwide reach. Evaluate the cost compared with the amount of royalties you expect to receive.

But my advice is to stop. Breathe. Understand your priorities as a congregational songwriter.

CONGREGATIONAL SONGWRITER PRIORITIES

I would consider signing up for the free option (if you live in the US), the MLC, as a songwriter with the primary concern of making Jesus famous and getting your songs out to local churches. You can always decide to sign up for a larger international publishing administration strategy with a DRCA if your songs generate worldwide recognition.

It is important for the congregational songwriter to have their songs registered with CCLI, who collects fees from churches and distributes royalties for rights holders. They are the largest Christian song lyric and sheet music publisher in the world. They exist to distribute your songs to over 250,000 churches around the world.

> *It is important for the congregational songwriter to have their song registered with CCLI, who collects fees from churches and distributes royalties for rights holders.*

You may not be able to sign up with CCLI as an individual unless you have multiple songs and a planned reach for those songs. You can sign with your new, local, faith-based publisher who has a publisher membership with CCLI (see the concept of learning to be a congregational songwriter and flourishing in a songwriting community with like-minded songwriters in my book *The 5 Steps to Get Your Songs Heard: A Congregational Songwriting Plan* found at https://getyoursongsheard.com or https://books2read.com/stephenrobertcass).

Even if you already have an individual publisher membership with CCLI and you become a member of the new, local, faith-based and like-minded publisher, the right agreements will be in place to assure accountability and integrity.

Finally, I want to remind you to choose ASCAP, BMI, or SESAC as your PRO. These entities authorize CCS to license churches and ministries to perform and play the songs in their repertoires, and in turn pay their affiliated songwriters and publishers.

Figure 9 – Worship music

Christian Copyright Solutions

Their quest is to help churches and Christian ministries "do music right."

CCS PROVIDES LICENSES complementing the areas of the RSE that CCLI does not provide. While CCLI provides licenses that cover the instances of *reproduction* rights, CCS designed theirs for *performance* rights coverage.

(I will write about what CCLI offers in chapter 8).

Here's a quick recap of the RSE. The 37-word primary focus statement of copyright law regarding churches states that the following is *not* a violation of it:

> *"PERFORMANCE of a nondramatic literary or musical work or of a dramatico-musical work of a religious nature, or DISPLAY of a work, in the course of services at a place of worship or other religious assembly."*

From the root of understanding that no one in the US can use a copyrighted work in public except the company or person who owns those rights, understand that churches have been given a judicial pass on the infringement of:

- Two (out of six) of the exclusive rights of the copyright holder (performance and display) for
- Two (out of six) categories[1] of copyrighted works (nondramatic literary or music, and dramatico-musical work of a religious nature)

This exemption is granted during one type of event:

- In the course of services at a place of worship or other religious assembly

This means that churches—public spaces—enjoy the freedom of the *live performance,* even if it's pre-recorded, of the music they love, or the recital of poetry or text from books, but not plays or dramatic performances unless they are purely religious.

It also means that they can *display* the lyrics or text of that work.

Although churches are exempt from infringement of two of the exclusive rights of a copyright holder, performance and display during services, they are *not* exempt from any other use or in any other situation. They have the same obligation as any other public place in the US when copyrighted music is performed and not covered by the RSE.[2]

These include music on hold, retreats, youth events, coffee shops, concerts, background music, and other special events—including the retransmission of the service and other gatherings. CCS provides licenses for those occasions when churches need coverage for performance of copyrighted songs outside of services. They partner with three PROs in the US: ASCAP, BMI, and SESAC, who represent more than 28 million songs from the songwriter and publisher members of those PROs.

CCS offers two licenses, the:

1. PERFORMmusic Facilities license, allowing your church to play or perform any song from the catalogs of ASCAP, BMI, or SESAC anywhere in your property or satellite campuses
2. WORSHIPcast streaming license. Your church may stream your services or any other special event, whether live or on-demand, from the *church-owned* website or *sponsored* url

The following graphic shows that the revenue generated by CCS flows to songwriters and copyright owners through PROs in the US. Specifically, ASCAP, BMI, and SESAC.

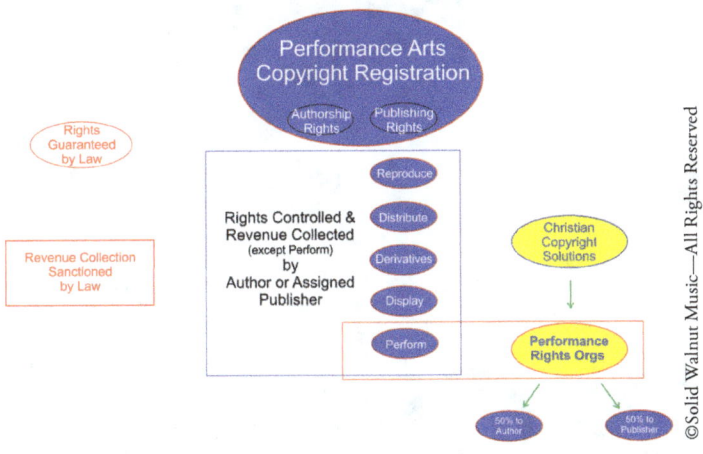

Figure 10 – How CCS pays royalties to song rights holder

Find them at https://christiancopyrightsolutions.com.

7

One License

Inspiring congregational song

OL IS A LEADING MUSIC LICENSE AGENCY for sacred and liturgical songs jointly owned by GIA Publications and the Oregon Catholic Press. Serving the US, Canada, The United Kingdom, Ireland, Australia, New Zealand, and Europe, they are a single resource that primarily serves Roman Catholic and traditional Protestant communities.

More than 25,000 global churches, schools, retreat centers, religious communities, funeral homes, and campus ministries have licenses with OL for the permissions to download tens of thousands of songs and thousands of images that can be inserted into worship aids, projection slides, and bulletins.

They have a growing list of over three hundred publishers who provide website links that make up the OL resource library for licensees. The member catalogs represent more than 80,000 songs, and users can download and report song usage at their website, https://onelicense.net.

Like CCLI, OL dedicates their licensing efforts toward the *reproduction* of copyrighted works. Their primary product is a license to reprint and project copyrighted lyrics.

The RSE exemption for the display of copyrighted lyrics speaks only to the actual display of the words, not to any means to store or to transmit the work. The Reprint license from OL covers such necessary copying.

They also offer two forms of Podcast/Streaming licenses because the RSE does not exempt the re-transmission of copyrighted music and lyrics.

A Practice-Track license, enabling pastors to create mp3s or CDs to distribute for the musicians or the choir, rounds out their license products.

ONE LICENSE OFFERINGS

Reprint License

For creating a display or using an electronic storage and retrieval system for the projection of words or music from member publishers and their catalogs.

- Not intended for the use of reprints for the choir, cantor, ensemble, instrumentalists, or accompanists
- Available in annual, single-use, or special events (up to 7 days)
- Allows reprints for your congregational or organizational use
    - Worship aids
    - Bulletins
    - Programs
    - Order of service

- Song sheet or song book
  - No sharing or selling is allowed

PODCAST/STREAMING LICENSE

Available in two forms. The more expansive of the two, a bundle including the Reprint license, allows the broadcasting of music and melody lines and encompasses all printing of congregational worship aids (although some publishers will not allow the rebroadcasting of their materials. Please verify permissions against your intended use).

The limited version is for those churches and organizations who wish to broadcast their services, though they don't use music or reprinting. Content for either license allows for streaming to the organization's website or to social media.

- Covers content only from live worship services
  - The retransmission of commercial masters or tracks can only be permitted with the consent of the copyright owner
- The number of views is limited to 3x your average weekly attendance
- While most publisher members allow their catalog to be streamed, some do not, so consult the OL member list
- The OL license number will need to be displayed during the service or linked to the podcast/livestream

As you might guess, there are many more caveats to read! It's not the fault of OL. Copyright law is quite specific regarding streaming. I will introduce more information about streaming in the next chapter.

PRACTICE-TRACK LICENSE

Practice-Track licenses are for music leaders to create recordings and duplications from member publisher catalogs for musicians and vocalists.

- Copying from member demos or from purchased commercial CDs/mp3 is allowed
- Recording the work into separate parts or arrangements for the purpose of education is ok
- Distributions by direct emailing or the use of Google Drive/Dropbox with limited access is required

One License distributes royalties directly to their member composers, authors, and publishers.

For more information, see https://us.ccli.com/ccli-news/ccli-onelicense/ and https://onelicense.net/options-and-prices.

Christian Copyright Licensing International

Understanding the many copyright issues related to music is complicated. We are here to make it easy.

CCLI LARGELY REPRESENTS a different set of music publishers than OL. Generally, CCLI presents modern worship songs. However, there is some overlap with songs from sacred and liturgical music publishers. CCLI has over 4000 major and independent publishers and song catalogs, with over 100,000 songs from those catalogs shown in SongSelect®, their online lyric, melody, and chord chart song service.

CCLI currently has licenses issued to over 250,000 churches around the world. There are over 160,000 churches licensed in North America.

ABOUT STREAMING

The following is the contrast between CCLI's *streaming* offerings and the offerings of both CCS and OL:

> Streaming is the broadcasting of copyrighted works which can infringe on all six exclusive rights of the copyright holder (reproduction, distribution, create derivatives, display, performance, and the right to digitally transmit sound recordings), which is why you will see extensive exclusions and caveats listed under the offerings from each company. You can think of streaming as the possible exposure of a right holder's entire copyright.
>
> CCS designed licenses to cover church *performances* outside of the worship service. OL has offerings regarding *reproduction* licensing. But both entities offer forms of streaming licenses. CCLI began licensing churches with *reproduction* licenses, but now offers two levels of streaming licenses, as does OL. The basic streaming license permissions will be similar to OL's. As is with OL, the live stream can only be *in the course of* services, but the difference between the offerings of the two companies is that CCLI allows the use of master recordings/tracks when streaming and OL does not. Or to better distinguish, CCLI will allow the use of the recordings *if* the ownership of them is from a member publisher. OL simply states that their license doesn't cover the use of it, and if

you intend to use recordings, *you* must seek permission from the copyright owner.

Again to distinguish, the streaming offering from CCS is for the use of songs in the ASCAP, BMI, and SESAC catalogs for any church event *outside* of services.

A bit of clarity on the larger discussion of the re-transmission of works: While the RSE *does* provide exemption for the performance of pre-recorded copyrighted works *in the course of services*, it *does not* provide exemption for the re-transmission of those works. So, it follows that CCS—who offers licenses for church events outside of services—does not offer them (at this date) for the re-transmission of commercial accompaniment tracks or other recordings.

Since re-transmission of commercial recordings is not exempt in churches, OL does not offer it with their streaming licenses. They state that you must secure individual permissions with copyright holders if you intend to stream these.

You may re-transmit commercial recordings such as backing and accompaniment tracks with a premium streaming license from CCLI, but *only* if the work is covered by works in a listed member catalog. Works outside their catalogs would require written permission to be re-transmitted.

LICENSES OFFERED FROM CCLI

Streaming

- Stream live and upload post-live recorded worship service songs to the website of the church or any streaming platform, as well as to any social media
  - If posting to YouTube or a similar service, all copyright guidelines from that platform must be followed
- There can be no fees charged for any use of the stream
- The stream can only be for the church service and not any other activity
- Any desired songs used must be verified as from a publisher member catalog
- All writer credits, copyright, and streaming license information must be posted for each song

Streaming Plus

Has all features of the Streaming license, but with the permission to use commercial master recordings and/or tracks during your service.

Church Copyright License®

- Access lyrics through SongSelect
- Copy songs from any known source to assist congregational singing
- Print songs in any manner for worship aids to prepare for congregational worship services such as bulletins and song sheets

- Store and retrieve song files for visual projection
- Record the songs in the live worship service for shut-ins and missionaries
  - The quantity reproduced cannot exceed 15% of your church license size
  - the songs used for the service may not be reproduced if accompaniment tracks or commercial recordings are used in the service (unless you receive direct approval from copyright holders)

Church Video License® and ScreenVue® Vault

CCLI has a partnership with Christian Video Licensing International (CVLI) and the Motion Picture Licensing Corporation (MPLC) to offer movie scenes or full-length movies for video needs during services or for any other church activity. ScreenVue® Vault, an extensive online resource, is the result.

A note that this license does not cover illegally obtained media nor allows charging admission fees.

Rehearsal License

CCLI issues this license solely for learning and rehearsing covered songs for a church with an active license. It allows worship leaders and musicians to stream, download, record, or make copies of commercial recordings of the covered songs for practices and rehearsals.

RESOURCES

SongSelect®

This is the online library of over 100,000 song lyrics and mp3 clips from publisher members. It offers transposable chord, lead, and vocal sheets and offers free access to any of their song resources in the public domain.

The chord sheets offer the selection between three different chord name systems and one alternate page layout.

The premium version offers a ChordPro® download option for chord sheets—a chord and musical instruction tool for worship leaders and musicians.

SongSelect® integrates with third-party tools that are popular, some might say essential, with worship teams: Planning Center Online, Presenter, and OnSong.

SongSelect® Liturgy Planning is a search engine and planning tool designed to simplify planning songs for Mass and for the liturgical calendar. It suggests modern, traditional, hymns, chants, and sacred songs applicable to the week of the calendar, responsorial psalms and Mass and liturgy settings. The same transposition and download options are available with this tool.

WorshipFuel

WorshipFuel is a completely free and deep video vault for musicians and worship leaders. Full of technical and musical tools for the worship service, WorshipFuel provides instructional videos on songwriting, vocal technique and care, and helpful technical gear. Many popular and upcoming songwriters, musicians, and worship leaders perform new and alternate versions of their songs, tutorials, testimony, and opinion on ways to establish and enhance a culture of worship.

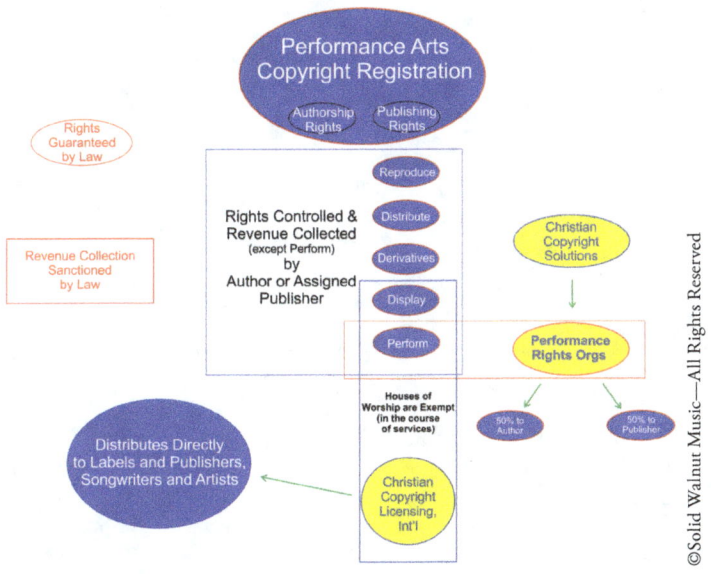

Figure 11 – CCLI pays royalties directly to song rights holders and CCS pays them through PROs.

Even though the above graphic shows that CCLI is paying rights holders for performance, they really aren't. CCLI collects from churches for copying and distributing. But in essence, their payments to rights holders compensate for the performance royalty revenue not generated because of the RSE.

Final Thoughts

WHY IT MATTERS

The confusion in our minds how to allocate resources fairly and wisely will always be with us. But it matters that we continually wrestle with it. The main character in our narrative, Jesus, understood our daily struggle. He tells us in many parables how we are better off and have clarity and are wiser in our money decisions when we try and take on the character of God.

Figure 12 – Jesus teaches about the character of God

We know that God wants our individual hearts to decide as we pray that his kingdom come, and his will be done on Earth as it is in Heaven. But what we often forget is that God is with us in the form of the Holy Spirit. We face the everyday resource struggle together. In silly business terms, God knows that we succeed when we seek the win-win. God doesn't need our money; he needs us to share it equitably.

The responses of Jesus to his challengers and the lesson of his parables contain ageless insights for us today. Our story arc of why it is important to pay for song IP speaks directly to the times when religious authorities tried to trap him with paying taxes. Payment of taxes is not good and right because it's a payment to Caesar and authorities, but because God is in command of all money, no matter where it's paid: To governments, authorities, or for goods and services. God wants *us* to be in control of where our hearts align as we determine where our money goes.

Since God owns all the cattle on a thousand hills, we certainly need to direct *our* hard-earned money towards those who also work hard for their money: The songwriters and publishers that make a living in service to their families or to expand their ministries.

In this labor of love that you have as a church leader, or as a songwriter with influence on church finances, my prayer is that you might see how God would favor the allocation of a portion of church money towards the songwriter and owner of IP. For a worker deserves their wage.

THE FUTURE OF CHURCH SONGWRITING

The future health of church ministries depend on the vibrancy of the ministries that provide strong spiritual songs and psalms to our communities.

My vision for songwriting in church, *The 5 Steps to Get Your Songs Heard*, found at https://getyoursongsheard.com and https://books2read.com/stephenrobertcass, contains a complete blueprint for local church songwriters to join or create like-minded songwriting communities to feed songs to local worship leaders. A local faith-based music publishing company is born in this plan to get the best songs from these writers out to the community and to the wider world. They use CCLI for song distribution, which works well for both local, national, and international exposure.

I and other song leaders who envision a strong songwriting community to serve churches in the future—whether these are teams internal to individual churches or are organized independently—advocate that worship services should not use only popular music but music from the grass roots—songs written for, from, and about your community. There is nothing wrong with songs that come from the music industry, but don't let the trend of only allowing popular songs in your churches block the influence of your local songwriter as they hear the voice of God. *Allow them to be his voice and nourish your community.*

Each community is special in their needs, praise, and *leadership*. Allow locally written and other songs to align with the message of the pastor to amplify local edification of the body of Christ.

Support paying songwriters and music publishers who write songs for church. Raise up your local musicians, technical crew, and songwriters and let them lead us into powerful, Spirit-led worship.

Figure 13 – Hands raised in praise

There's a unique power in a room dense with songs proclaiming the truth of the possibility of connecting with God. Strong singing in church is a witness to those who are seeking of how the children of God are unified around his story, and of how we respond to the outpouring of his undeserved kindness toward us.

What a testimony it is when visitors come to your church and hear the outpouring of praise! Impressions are usually formed by the music and how the congregation was singing. As songwriters, our job is to make sure they receive this sense of worship at every service. Helping others to build deep faith is not separate from congregational singing. It is a crucial part of a closer walk with God. People come to church in search of that closer walk.

Worship Songs & The Law

The congregational songwriter writes about the story of God, skillfully weaving in common emotions and experiences, creating a strong desire in the worshiper to sing his praise

Support your local and national songwriters so *all* ministries can grow. A healthy church is often determined by how healthy the music is in that church which then feeds and helps to sustain all ministries. We are drawn in by music. It is how we best communicate with each other and a wonderful tool to communicate our hearts to God.

> Let the message of Christ dwell among you richly as you teach and admonish one another with all wisdom through psalms, hymns, and songs from the Spirit, singing to God with gratitude in your hearts. And whatever you do, whether in word or deed, do it all in the name of the Lord Jesus, giving thanks to God the Father through him.
>
> — **Colossians 3:16-17**

CHURCH MUSIC LICENSE CHECK-UP

Does your church use songs or other worship aids that are IP? Do you plan to record your services for distribution? Are you planning to live stream your church service? Do you plan on live streaming any church activities that are not the main church service? Are there songs used in your youth ministries? Do you have a church coffee shop or use music on hold or play copyrighted music before or after service?

Do you have events scheduled outside of your services with the plan of performing copyrighted songs or distributing other copyrighted material?

Gather with church leadership to ask these exact questions so you can determine which type of church licensing is most appropriate. It is not uncommon to need a license from more than one of these companies. Take this physical book or digital copy to the meeting, or use this book to prepare a presentation, and use Chapters 6, 7, and 8 to see the licensing available to make your decisions. Know the basics of the Religious Service Exemption as outlined in copyright law as I summarized in Chapter 1 and at the beginning of Chapter 6.

And refer to the Endnotes section to find helpful comments and references in your learning journey.

Pray for the health of worship music and for churches around the world.

Figure 14 – Praying for churches around the world

Endnotes

Chapter 1

1. Please read this informative article: https://edensbridge.org/2012/01/11/on-justice-and-righteousness-mishpat-tsadaq-strongs-4941-6663/, and this supporting reference: https://bible.knowing-jesus.com/strongs/H6663. This important reference shows that *mishpat* in today's Hebrew language is the word for law and speaks to its roots. https://www.thejc.com/judaism/jewish-words/mishpat-1.8055
2. https://www.copyright.gov/registration/#types-of-works
3. https://geniemusic.com?w=1115
4. https://geniemusic.com?w=264
5. https://us.ccli.com/ccli-news/five-questions/
6. https://onelicense.net/about-us
7. https://www.beaconjournal.com/story/news/local/2020/08/22/lsquodifficult-days-are-aheadrsquo-for-americarsquos-churches-faith-institutions/42282593/
8. https://brill.com/view/book/edcoll/9789004412927/BP000016.xml
9. https://en.wikipedia.org/wiki/Religion_in_Mexico
10. https://library.cqpress.com/cqresearcher/document.php?id=cqresrre1926080100

11. https://christiancopyrightsolutions.com/blog/the-religious-service-exemption-explained/

Chapter 2

1. https://www.mtsu.edu/first-amendment/article/1072/copyright-act-of-1976
2. https://en.wikipedia.org/wiki/Copyright_Act_of_1909
3. https://us.ccli.com/about-ccli/history/
4. http://www.nytimes.com/1984/04/20/us/church-is-guilty-in-copyright-case.html
   https://www.chicagotribune.com/news/ct-xpm-1990-06-13-9002180039-story.html
5. https://us.ccli.com/what-we-provide/
6. https://us.ccli.com/about-ccli/history/
7. https://christiancopyrightsolutions.com/
8. https://onelicense.net/options-and-prices
9. https://christiancopyrightsolutions.com/questions/
10. https://caselaw.findlaw.com/us-5th-circuit/1641782.html
11. https://dockets.justia.com/docket/newyork/nyedce/1:2011cv05255/32355
12. https://law.justia.com/cases/federal/districtcourts/FSupp/789/823/1640963/
13. https://casetext.com/case/malaco-incorporated-v-cooper
14. https://law.justia.com/cases/federal/districtcourts/FSupp/789/823/1640963/
15. https://law.justia.com/cases/federal/districtcourts/FSupp/855/1314/1972870/
    A supporting article:
    https://churchleaders.com/worship/worship-articles/158121-why-smaller-churches-can-t-fly-under-the-copyright-radar.html

16. https://www.jdsupra.com/legalnews/congress-creates-a-small-claims-court-7022155/
17. https://www.copyright.gov/about/small-claims/ https://blogs.loc.gov/copyright/2021/12/the-case-act-copyright-claims-board-to-begin-hearing-cases-in-spring-2022/

Chapter 3

1. https://www.copyright.gov/what-is-copyright/
2. https://www.copyright.gov/circs/circ01.pdf
3. https://www.copyright.gov/fair-use/
4. https://www.copyright.gov/title17/92chap1.html#115
5. Each of these links are important if you are interested to hear the entire story from David Crowder and John Mark McMillan. Start with this video of David. https://www.youtube.com/watch?v=FjHDVDX8JF4 https://www.biola.edu/blogs/biola-magazine/2010/worship-creativity-and-a-sloppy-wet-kiss https://johnmarkmcmillan.wordpress.com/2009/09/14/how-he-loves-david-crowder-and-sloppy-wet-kisses/
6. This is great article that simplifies the complicated story of interpreting the rights of the copyright holder. In the digital age, it gets tough to interpret. Here, Genius wants to sue Google for ripping off Genius' content, but a three-judge panel in 2022 concludes that Genius doesn't own the lyrics to songs, artists do, and they are only creating a legal derivative in the first place. That's the right call in my book! https://9to5google.com/2022/03/14/google-genius-lyric-lawsuit/
7. Using copyrighted material on the internet is complicated. No matter the depth of your interest in

learning how YouTube works for copyright, please visit the first link, a YouTube company short video, which is an excellent explainer.
https://www.youtube.com/watch?v=6pgMtJHg9gg
https://support.google.com/youtube/answer/2797370?hl=en
https://www.tubefilter.com/2018/11/07/youtube-payouts-content-id/
https://support.google.com/youtube/answer/2853833?hl=en
https://www.tubics.com/blog/what-counts-as-a-view-on-youtube

Chapter 4

1. https://www.copyright.gov/circs/circ01.pdf
2. https://www.copyright.gov/help/faq/faq-general.html#poorman
3. https://www.copyright.gov/help/faq/faq-duration.html

Chapter 5

1. The legal world of copyright protection is over-complicated. The basis of copyright law says that performance rights need to be collected by the existing PROs. But as technology progressed, more and more "what ifs" emerged. The first link here is copyright law (read the #51 footnote to see how the law has changed) and the second link is a great overview of what is happening today.
   https://www.copyright.gov/title17/92chap1.html#115
   https://soundcharts.com/blog/performance-rights-organizations
2. https://www.soundexchange.com/who-we-are/#about-us
3. https://www.royaltyexchange.com/blog/the-songwriter-and-music-publisher-relationship-pt-4

4. https://www.ascap.com/help/royalties-and-payment/payment
   https://www.ascap.com/~/media/site-pages/annual-report/2021/ascap_annual-report_2021-compressed.pdf
5. https://www.copyright.gov/music-modernization/
   https://en.wikipedia.org/wiki/Music_Modernization_Act
6. https://www.themlc.com/our-story
7. https://christiancopyrightsolutions.com/learning center/
   https://apps.christiancopyrightsolutions.com/docs/factsheets/FactSheet-DifferenceBetweenCCLIandCCS.pdf

Chapter 6

1. https://www.copyright.gov/registration/#types-of-works
2. https://christiancopyrightsolutions.com/blog/the-religious-service-exemption-explained/

Other helpful websites for determining the situation of your church:

https://www.jwpepper.com/images/events/pdf/Church%20Copyright%20Webinar%20Q%20&%20A.pdf

https://blogs.jwpepper.com/copyright-for-virtual-worship-services-what-you-can-and-cannot-do/

https://us.ccli.com/ccli-news/ccli-onelicense/

https://onelicense.net/options-and-prices

https://christiancopyrightsolutions.com/

https://cvli.com

About the Author

Stephen Robert Cass is a hack golfer who aims for high mediocrity. Because of his lofty goals on the course, he may one day enter charity tournaments so he can donate his time and talents. When not swinging for the fences, he's known for:

- ❑ 50+ years as a worship musician and team member,
- ❑ 14 years as a worship leader,
- ❑ 27 years as a published Christian songwriter,
- ❑ 15 album projects, whether solo, produced or musician credits,
- ❑ 70+ worship song titles found at CCLI under the Solid Walnut Music catalog and Stephen Robert Cass.

Solid Walnut Music has given away original music CDs to Christian radio stations all over the world: the US, Canada, Mexico, Australia, England, Ireland, Russia, Ethiopia, Bulgaria, Italy, South Africa, South Korea, and Israel.

Go to https://getyoursongsheard.com, so your friends can receive this book plus bonuses.

Visit https://books2read.com/stephenrobertcass to find where his books are available.

See https://stephenrobertcass.com for all other e-book releases, the press kit, and speaking engagements.

Swing by https://songs4god.net for songwriting blogs and other information about Steve.

Please leave a review of this book at your favorite bookstore. Contact steve@songs4god.net.

www.ingramcontent.com/pod-product-compliance
Lightning Source LLC
Chambersburg PA
CBHW050308120526
44590CB00016B/2534